Virginia Fish Species
Game Fish & Panfish

Billy Grinslott – Kinsey Marie Books

ISBN - 9781968228460

Redear sunfish are known for their red or orange-edged gill flaps. They are a type of sunfish that thrive in warm, quiet waters, feeding primarily on mollusks and snails, and can grow up to 12 inches and weigh as much as 2 pounds. They are also known as shellcracker, due to their diet and the way they crush shells. The redear sunfish will thrive in most warm-water lakes and streams.

The Flier is a small, sunfish known for its olive-green color, rows of dark spots, and a dark teardrop or streak below its eye, with large dorsal and anal fins. It inhabits slow-moving, clear waters in the Southern U.S. coastal plains and Mississippi river basin. They feed on insects, snails, worms, leeches, crustaceans, and small fish, also some phytoplankton.

The bluegill also considered a sunfish is the most popular fish to fish for. They are called pan fish because they are about the size of a frying pan. Bluegills love to eat insects and bugs. They have good vision and rely on their keen eyesight to feed. Three types in this group are the Bluegill, Sunfish, and Pumpkinseed.

The Redbreast sunfish has a red-yellow chest and belly with rusty brown spots on their body. The species is known for its distinctive grunting vocalizations, which are produced by grinding their teeth together. Redbreast sunfish can survive in oxygen-poor environments by using their gills to extract oxygen from air bubbles trapped in aquatic vegetation.

The Blue spotted sunfish is a small freshwater fish known for its vibrant blue spots and tolerance for acidic low oxygen waters. They are native to the southeastern and eastern United States, inhabiting ponds, rivers, and backwaters with dense vegetation. They are one of the smallest fish in their family, typically reaching a maximum length of about 3.7 inches. Both males and females have light blue or white spots, but males tend to have more intense and vibrant spotting. They have a relatively short lifespan, typically living around 5 years.

The Green Sunfish is blue green in color. It has yellow flecks on both its scales and some parts of its sides. The Green Sunfish also has broken blue stripes which is why some people confuse it with the Bluegill. Green Sunfish are very adaptable. They can live in any body of water that has vegetation or weeds. Green sunfish are opportunistic feeders, consuming insects, small fish, and other invertebrates.

Banded Sunfish got their name because they have darker lines that run vertically on their sides. They also have a rounded tail with spots on their body, tail and fins. Banded sunfish are typically only about 2 inches long, making them one of the smallest sunfish. Their small size makes them vulnerable to larger fish, so they thrive in protected areas. Banded sunfish prefer slow-moving, vegetated waters like swamps, ponds, and backwaters of creeks

The Pumpkinseed is also known as pond perch, sun perch, and punky's sunfish. It can be found in numerous lakes, ponds, and rivers. It is their body shape resembling the seed of a pumpkin, that inspired their name. Pumpkinseed sunfish have speckles on their orangish colored sides and back, with a yellow to orange belly and chest. They are active during the day and rest at night near the bottom or in shelter areas.

A Roanoke bass is a rare, native sunfish, related to rock bass. It's known for its dark olive-green color or smaller spots. It prefers to live in clean, flowing water in creeks and small rivers with rocky bottoms but is sensitive to siltation. While similar to the common rock bass, Roanoke bass have fewer, smaller spots and scaleless cheeks, along with a slightly concave forehead, making them distinct.

The Rock Bass is not actually a bass but a member of the sunfish family. They are often called red eye or goggle eye due to their distinctive bright red eyes. The biggest Rock Bass ever caught on record weighs about three pounds and was a little over one foot long. Rock bass prefer waters with rocky vegetated areas, that's how they got their name.

The Warmouth is a member of the Rock Bass, Green Sunfish and Bluegill family. They can survive in low oxygen environments while other fish cannot. Warmouth can thrive in muddy water, when other fish can't. Warmouth are often confused with rock bass. The difference between the two is in the anal fin: warmouth have three spines on the anal fin ray and rock bass have six spines.

The Blackbanded Sunfish is a small, deep-bodied freshwater fish known for its striking 6 bold black vertical bars, small mouth, and colorful pelvic fins. It prefers to live in calm, shallow, waters with dense aquatic plants in swamps, ponds, and slow streams. They are omnivores, eating small invertebrates and plants, and are considered a cold-water fish, unlike many common sunfish. They are small, usually under 4 inches long.

The two most famous perches are the common perch and the yellow perch. The yellow perch has a brilliant greenish yellow color with orange fins. The yellow perch is the biggest one and can grow to a size of 18 inches. It's also known as the jumbo perch. The other type of perch is the white perch. The biggest yellow perch caught in Virginia was a 3-pound monster with a length of 16.5 inches

White perch grow seven to ten inches in length and rarely weigh more than one pound. They have a silvery body with faint lines on the sides. The white perch is an opportunistic feeder. Young feed primarily on zooplankton and adults feed on aquatic insect larvae, minnows and fish eggs. White Perch is a euryhaline species, inhabiting fresh, brackish and coastal waters. The biggest White Perch caught in Virginia weighed 3 pounds, 2 ounces.

The Roanoke logperch is a colorful, bottom-dwelling darter fish known for flipping rocks with its snout to feed on mayflies and caddisflies in clear, gravelly water. A Roanoke logperch is a small, typically growing to about 6 inches long, with some reaching up to 8 inches. They're known for multiple bright colors, especially orange bands on their fins in males, and distinct blotches on their bodies.

There are two main types of crappies. The white crappie and the black crappie. They are also members of the sunfish family. The difference between the white and black crappie is one has dark spots and the other has dark lines and is lighter in color. The white crappie has six dorsal fin spines, whereas the black crappie has eight dorsal fin spines. The white crappie can grow bigger and more of the bigger white crappie are caught in North America. The official Virginia state record by weight is a 4-pound 14-ounce crappie.

Bowfins can breathe both air and water, putting them at an advantage in low-oxygen waters. Bowfins are often described as prehistoric relics. This is because species can be traced to fossils from the Cretaceous, Eocene and Jurassic period. The biggest Bowfin caught in Virginia weighed 17 pounds, 8 ounces.

There are few different species of Gar, the Longnose gar, Short nose and Alligator gar. The Long Nose Gar got its name because of its long mouth that looks like an alligator's mouth. The alligator gar is one of the biggest freshwater fish growing up to 10 feet long. The world record for a catch was set at 327 pounds. The biggest confirmed Gar caught in Virginia by weight is a 23-pound Longnose Gar.

Redhorse are large, bottom-feeding freshwater sucker fish known for their reddish fins, and molar-like throat teeth that they use to crush mollusks. They inhabit in clear rivers with gravelly bottoms, where they feed on insects and detritus. They spawn in spring, often migrating upstream. They are popular with anglers for their strong fight, when catching them in swift currents. They can grow to around 18 pounds and 30 inches long.

Male freshwater drum make a rumbling or grunting sound by contracting muscles along their air bladder walls. They have large, ivory-like ear bones that can be up to an inch in diameter, which Native Americans used as necklaces or bracelets and sometimes referred to as the lucky stones. Freshwater drum are primarily bottom feeders, spending much of their time near the bottom of lakes and rivers in search of food. The biggest freshwater drum caught in Virginia, weighed 29 pounds, 6 ounces.

Carp have long been an important food fish to humans. Carp are bottom feeders for the most part and their mouth is made like a suction cup, so they can suck food off the bottom. Carp are good for a lake because they help clean the bottom of the lake. Carp are introduced for aquatic vegetation control and can grow very large. The biggest Common Carp officially recorded in Virginia weighed 49 pounds 4 ounces.

The black, brown and yellow bullhead are part of the catfish family. They usually only grow to about 10 inches long. They use their whiskers to help find food. The bullhead is the most common member of the catfish family. Bullheads live in the water containing low oxygen levels. They can survive on low oxygen areas, where other fish can't. Virginia's biggest bullhead record appears to be a recent Brown Bullhead weighing 5.45 pounds.

White catfish are interesting because they are smaller than other common catfish species like channel catfish, they have a wider head and lack the black spots of channel catfish. White catfish are the smallest of the large North American catfish species. The White catfish has white chin barbells, which distinguish it from other species. There are four pairs of barbels, whiskers around the mouth, two on the chin, one at the angle of the mouth, and one behind the nostril. The biggest White Catfish caught in Virginia weighed 7 lbs. 6 oz.

Flathead Catfish, their body is wide but flattened and very low in height. Both eyes are on the top of the flattened head, giving excellent vision to see upward. Flathead catfish live mainly in large bodies of water like big rivers and reservoirs. They prefer deep pools of water. The biggest Flathead Catfish officially recorded in Virginia weighed 68 pounds, 12 ounces.

The Channel Catfish are the most fished catfish species with around 8 million anglers fishing for them per year. Channel catfish have taste buds all over their body, making them highly sensitive to the taste and smell of food. They also have barbels (whiskers) around their mouths, which are used for sensing and tasting food. They use sound waves to communicate with each other. They can also produce alarm substances to warn other catfish of danger. The biggest Channel Catfish caught in Virginia weighed 31 pounds, 8 ounces.

Blue catfish are known for their size, reaching over 100 pounds. Blue catfish, like other catfish, lack scales and have smooth skin. They have barbels (whiskers) around their mouths, which are used for sensing and tasting food. They are generally slate blue on the back and silvery/white on the underside. The biggest blue catfish ever caught in Virginia was a massive 143-pounder.

White Bass or striped bass range in color from a silvery white to a pale green. Their backs are mostly black, while their sides and belly are pale with stripes running along them. White Bass are related to Striped Bass and sometimes called wipers. The general world record for a white bass is around 6.8 pounds.

The Hybrid Striped Bass is a cross between a male White Bass and a female Striped Bass, known for its broken stripes, deep body, and excellent fighting ability. It's a favorite game fish in many freshwater reservoirs, prized for its aggressive nature, often caught with spoons, jigs, or live bait, especially in cooler months. They are sterile and do not reproduce naturally, so they are stocked in lakes and rivers by state hatcheries. They can grow to significant sizes, often reaching several pounds within three years. The biggest Hybrid Striped Bass (Wiper) caught in Virginia, and the current state record, is 15 pounds, 13 ounces.

Striped bass are often called Stripers. Striped bass live in both salt and fresh water. Striped bass have very sensitive eyes and will seek deep water when the sun is out. Striped bass have a preferred water temperature range of from 55° F to 68° F, and swim to find water of these temperatures. White Bass are related to Striped Bass and have lighter stripes on their sides. The biggest Striped Bass caught in Virginia, and the official state record, is a massive 74-pounder.

Spotted bass have rows of dark spots on their sides and an iridescent green pattern along their back. Spotted bass are also known as Kentucky's or redeye bass. They are a popular game fish, often mistaken for largemouth bass, but they have subtle differences like a a smaller mouth. They are known for their aggressive nature and tendency to school together. They also prefer rocky bottoms and being in deeper water compared to other bass who like shallow water. The biggest officially recognized Spotted Bass in Virginia weighed 4 pounds, 7 ounces.

The largemouth bass is the most sought-after bass in North America. Largemouth bass live in just about every lake in North America. They have great hearing and can hear a crayfish crawling on the bottom of the lake. The biggest largemouth bass caught in Virginia weighed 16 pounds, 4 ounces.

A golden largemouth bass is an exceptionally rare variation of the common bass, distinguished by its vibrant yellow or gold color, caused by a genetic condition called xanthism, where normal dark pigments are suppressed, allowing yellow pigments to dominate, making them highly prized catches that are usually released back into the water.

Smallmouth bass have a smaller mouth than the largemouth bass. They also have different markings and are lighter in color. They don't live in most lakes because they prefer living in colder water. They are typically found in the northern states in America because the water is cooler. The current world record smallmouth is an 11-pound, 15-ounce fish caught in Dale Hollow Lake. The biggest Smallmouth Bass caught in Virginia weighed 8 pounds, 1 ounce.

Alabama bass are a type of black bass, that are native to the Mobile River basin in Alabama, Georgia, and Mississippi. They are often mistaken for Spotted bass but are more elongated and tend to weigh less per inch. A key characteristic is a dark, blotchy lateral band from head to tail with spots below the band. Alabama bass prefer clear, deep water with rocky substrates, and are less common in turbid waters or areas with sand or mud substrates.

Sturgeons have sharp spines on their back, so be careful when handling them. Instead of scales, sturgeon skin is covered in bony plates called scutes, which can be very sharp on young sturgeon. Sturgeons have been around since the dinosaur days. Sturgeons mostly live in large, freshwater lakes and rivers. Their average lifespan is 50 to 60 years. They can grow to be quite large, with some reaching 6-8 feet long and weighing up to 300 pounds.

Paddlefish are among the oldest surviving fish species in North America, dating back to about 125 million years ago. Their most distinctive feature is their long, flat, paddle-shaped snout, which helps them detect and locate tiny aquatic creatures. Paddlefish are true bottom-dwelling creatures, that are hard to catch, and can grow to weigh over 160 pounds.

Snakehead fish are known as walking fish, because they can move on land for days by wiggling with their fins and body. They can breathe air with lung-like organs, allowing them to survive out of water for days and even crawl to new water bodies using their fins. They can also burrow into the mud and hibernate during cold weather or dry spells. They thrive in various slow-moving, shallow, vegetated waters, like ponds, swamps, and streams, and can survive in low oxygen levels. The largest snakehead fish caught in Virginia, is a 19-pound, 5-ounce northern snakehead.

The sauger is part of the walleye family. There are 2 different types of saugers. The normal sauger and the suageye. The saugeye is a mix of the sauger and walleye. The suageye have white eyes just like the walleye. The sauger and suageye are smaller than the walleye. Saugers are more likely to be found in large rivers with deep pools but are also found in lakes. The largest saugeye caught in Virginia is a 6-pound, 8-ounce trophy.

The walleye got its name because of its white looking eyes. Their eyes collect light, even in low light conditions. This means they can see in the dark. Because they can see in the dark, they mostly feed at night. During the daytime their eyes are very sensitive, so they usually head for deeper water or shady places. Walleye like to live in cooler water and are normally found in the upper part of North America. The largest walleye ever caught in Virginia was a historic, unofficial record of 23.5 pounds.

Pickerel, also called pike, look like northern pike, but they are not. The Pike is larger in size than the Pickerel. The Pickerel has more spots than the Pike, but the Pike has spots on its fins and pickerel don't. The Pickerel has a dark bar beneath their eyes and northern pike don't. There are 2 types of Pickerel, Chain Pickerel, and Redfin Pickerel. The largest official Chain Pickerel state record in Virginia, is 7 pounds, 2 ounces.

The Northern Pike is one of the most sought-after fish for anglers. It got its name because it likes to live in cooler water mainly in the northern states of North America. The northern pike is a very aggressive predator. They don't like to live in groups with other fish, they are very territorial and like to live alone. Their behavior is closely affected by weather conditions. The largest Northern Pike caught in Virginia weighed 31 pounds, 4 ounces.

The muskellunge called the Musky or Muskie for short is one of the biggest game fish in freshwater lakes. They are hard to catch, they say it takes a thousand casts to catch one. They're stocked and sought by anglers in these connected cool-water river systems. Muskellunge (Muskie) are primarily found in the western mountain rivers like the New, Nolichucky, and French Broad Rivers, and reservoirs such as Fontana and Lake Adger and Hiwassee. The largest muskellunge (musky) recorded in Virginia weighed 45 pounds, 8 ounces.

Brown trout can live up to 20 years. Brown exhibits a variety of colors and spotting patterns, with red spots surrounded by blue halos and black spots being common. Brown trout have higher tolerance for warmer waters than either the brook or rainbow trout. Brown trout can be found on almost every continent except Antarctica. The largest brown trout ever caught in Virginia weighed 18 pounds, 11 ounces.

Brook trout are characterized by their olive-green bodies with pale, worm-like markings, red spots with bluish halos, and orange-red fins with white and black edges. They can grow up to 12 inches in length. Brook trout are cold-water fish that prefer clean, clear, and cold streams, lakes, and ponds. The largest Brook Trout caught in Virginia weighed 5 pounds, 15 ounces.

The rainbow trout gets its name because of its brilliant colors. Rainbow trout populations are good indicators of water pollution because they can only survive in clean waters. They like to live in rivers and streams. Rainbow trout rank among the top five most sought game fish in North America. The largest rainbow trout caught in Virginia, weighed 14 pounds, 12 ounces.

Interesting Fish Facts in Virginia.

1 - Virginia boasts over 220 freshwater fish species, including diverse game fish like bass, catfish, and trout.

2 - The native Brook Trout is Virginia's state freshwater fish, thriving in cold mountain streams.

3 - Popular game fish include Largemouth Bass, Smallmouth Bass, and Black Crappie.

4 - The biggest freshwater fish ever caught in Virginia is a massive 143-pound Blue Catfish.

5 - The smallest freshwater fish caught in Virginia is likely the Least Killifish, only 2 inches long.

6 - Species like Channel and Blue Catfish lack scales and use "whiskers" (barbels) with taste buds to find food on the bottom.

7 - Largemouth Bass are a popular target for anglers, with rare genetic golden variants found.

8 - Striped Bass, known locally as rockfish, are a prized catch in both freshwater and saltwater.

Author Page

Billy Grinslott – Kinsey Marie Books

Copyright, All Rights Reserved

ISBN – 9781968228460

Thanks

www.ingramcontent.com/pod-product-compliance
Lightning Source LLC
Chambersburg PA
CBHW060848270326
41934CB00002B/43